# Little Big Giant

### Stories of Wisdom and Inspiration

# Cher

*Goddess of Pop*

# Introduction

In the summer of 1986, the world was captivated by the mysterious disappearance of pop icon, Cher. The beloved singer and actress had just finished filming her latest movie, "Moonstruck," and was set to embark on a sold-out concert tour. However, just days before the tour was set to begin, Cher vanished without a trace.

Rumors swirled about her whereabouts, with some speculating that she had been kidnapped or even killed. The media frenzy only intensified when a ransom note was discovered, demanding an exorbitant amount of money for Cher's safe return.

As the days turned into weeks, the public became increasingly obsessed with the case, with everyone from fans to law enforcement trying to piece together what had happened to the beloved star. Despite numerous leads and potential suspects, Cher remained missing, leaving the world wondering if they would ever see her again.

But just when all hope seemed lost, a shocking twist in the case emerged. Cher was found alive and well, but with no memory of the past few weeks. To this day, the events surrounding her disappearance remain a mystery, leaving many to wonder what truly happened to the enigmatic superstar.

As the world continues to be fascinated by Cher's disappearance, one question remains: will the truth ever be revealed? Only time will tell in this gripping tale of fame, mystery, and the enduring power of one of the most iconic figures in pop culture history.

# Table of Contents

# Chapter 1

*Childhood and Early Beginnings*

Cher was born on May 20th, 1946 in El Centro, California. Her parents, Georgia Holt and John Sarkisian, were both struggling actors at the time. Cher's birth name was actually Cherilyn Sarkisian, but she later legally changed it to just Cher.

Growing up, Cher had a very difficult childhood. Her parents divorced when she was just 10 months old and she was raised primarily by her mother. Georgia struggled to make ends meet and often had to work multiple jobs to support Cher and her older half-sister, Georganne. This meant that Cher spent a lot of time alone and often felt neglected.

Despite the challenges she faced, Cher was a natural performer from a young age. She loved to sing and dance, and would often put on shows for her family and friends. Her mother recognized her talent and encouraged her to pursue a career in entertainment.

At the age of 16, Cher dropped out of high school and moved to Los Angeles with her friend, where she began taking acting and singing lessons. She also started performing in small clubs and coffee shops, honing her skills and gaining experience.

**Key Takeaway:** Even though Cher faced many challenges in her childhood, she never let them hold her back from pursuing her dreams. She worked hard and never gave up, which ultimately led to her success in the entertainment industry.

13

# Chapter 2

*Rising to Fame with Sonny and Cher*

Cher was a young girl with big dreams and a voice that could light up any room. She loved to sing and perform, and she knew that one day she would make it big. Little did she know, her journey to fame would begin when she met a young man named Sonny.

Sonny was a musician and songwriter who saw something special in Cher. He believed in her talent and wanted to help her reach her full potential. Together, they formed the musical duo, Sonny and Cher, and their rise to fame was just beginning.

Their first big break came when they were signed to a record label and released their hit song, "I Got You Babe." It quickly became a sensation and topped the charts all over the world. People couldn't get enough of Sonny and Cher's unique sound and their chemistry on stage.

As their popularity grew, so did their opportunities. They were invited to perform on popular TV shows and even had their own variety show, "The Sonny and Cher Comedy Hour." Their dynamic performances and witty banter captured the hearts of audiences everywhere.

But with fame also came challenges. Cher and Sonny faced criticism and backlash for their unconventional style and outspoken personalities. However, they didn't let it stop them from pursuing their dreams and continuing to make music that they loved.

Despite the ups and downs, Sonny and Cher's success only continued to grow. They released more hit songs like "The Beat Goes On" and "All I Ever Need Is You." They also became fashion icons, known for their bold and unique style.

**Key Takeaway:** Sometimes, the people we meet and the opportunities we are given can change our lives in ways we never imagined. Cher's collaboration with Sonny not only led to their success as a musical duo, but it also taught her the importance of believing in herself and never giving up on her dreams.

# Chapter 3

## Solo Career and "Believe" Breakthrough

After years of success with her duo Sonny and Cher, Cher decided to embark on a solo career in the late 1970s. She was determined to prove herself as a strong and independent artist, and she did just that.

Cher's first solo album, "Cher," was released in 1979 and received positive reviews. She continued to release albums throughout the 1980s, experimenting with different styles and genres. However, it wasn't until 1998 that Cher had her biggest breakthrough with the release of her hit single "Believe."

"Believe" was a dance-pop song that showcased Cher's powerful vocals and unique style. It became an instant hit, topping the charts in over 20 countries and earning Cher her first Grammy Award. The song also introduced a new music technology called Auto-Tune, which Cher used to enhance her vocals and create a distinctive sound.

The success of "Believe" not only solidified Cher's solo career but also made her the oldest female artist to have a number one hit on the Billboard Hot 100 chart. At 52 years old, she proved that age was just a number and that she was still a force to be reckoned with in the music industry.

Cher's music video for "Believe" also made waves, with its futuristic and edgy aesthetic. It was one of the first music videos to use computer-generated imagery and was praised for its creativity and innovation.

With the success of "Believe," Cher continued to release hit albums and singles, cementing her status as a music icon. She also ventured into other areas of entertainment, such as acting and producing, and became a well-rounded and versatile artist.

**Key Takeaway:** Cher's solo career and the breakthrough success of "Believe" showed that determination, hard work, and staying true to oneself can lead to great achievements. It also proved that age is not a barrier to success, and one can continue to grow and evolve as an artist throughout their career.

# Chapter 4

## Acting Career and Oscar Win for "Moonstruck"

Cher's acting career began to take off in the 1980s with her role in the film "Silkwood." This led to more opportunities, including her iconic role as Loretta Castorini in the romantic comedy "Moonstruck."

In "Moonstruck," Cher played a widow who falls in love with her fiance's younger brother. Her performance was praised by critics and audiences alike, earning her an Academy Award for Best Actress in 1988. This made her the first and only female artist to win an Oscar, a Grammy, an Emmy, and a Golden Globe.

But Cher's success didn't stop there. She continued to star in popular films such as "Mermaids," "The Witches of Eastwick," and "Mask." She also showed her versatility as an actress by taking on more serious roles in films like "Suspect" and "Tea with Mussolini."

Despite her success in Hollywood, Cher faced challenges as a woman in the industry. She often had to fight for equal pay and roles that were not stereotypical. But she never let these obstacles stop her from pursuing her passion for acting.

**Key Takeaway:** Cher's Oscar win for "Moonstruck" not only made her the first female artist to achieve EGOT status, but it also showed that women can be powerful and successful in the entertainment industry. She proved that with hard work and determination, anything is possible.

# Chapter 5

*Personal Life and Relationships*

Cher was not only a talented singer and actress, but she also had a very interesting personal life. She was married twice and had many high-profile relationships throughout her career.

Cher's first marriage was to singer Sonny Bono, who she met when she was just 16 years old. They formed the famous duo "Sonny and Cher" and had a successful music career together. They were married for 11 years and had one child, Chaz Bono. However, their marriage ended in divorce in 1975.

After her divorce from Sonny, Cher had several relationships with famous men, including musician Gregg Allman and actor Val Kilmer. She also had a brief romance with actor Tom Cruise. However, it wasn't until 1986 that she found love again with record executive Rob Camilletti. Despite their 18-year age difference, they were together for three years and even lived together.

In 1998, Cher married for the second time to musician and actor, Sonny Bono's former partner, Gregg Allman. However, their marriage only lasted four years before they divorced in 2002.

Aside from her marriages, Cher also had a close relationship with her mother, Georgia Holt. They even appeared together in a documentary called "Dear Mom, Love Cher" in 2013. Cher's mother was also a singer and had a big influence on her daughter's career.

**Key Takeaway:** Cher's personal life was filled with ups and downs, but she always remained strong and focused on her career. She also had a close relationship with her mother, who played a significant role in shaping her as a person and an artist.

# Chapter 6

*Comeback with "If I Could Turn Back Time"*

Cher had been in the music industry for decades, and she had seen it all. From the highs of fame and success to the lows of personal struggles and criticism, she had weathered it all. But nothing could have prepared her for the challenge she faced in the early 1980s - a career slump.

After a string of successful albums and hit singles, Cher's popularity began to decline. She struggled to find her footing in the ever-changing music scene and her record sales were plummeting. It seemed like her time in the spotlight was coming to an end.

But Cher was not one to give up easily. She took some time off to reflect and reassess her career. And then, in 1989, she made her comeback with the iconic song "If I Could Turn Back Time."

The song was a huge success, reaching number three on the Billboard Hot 100 chart and becoming Cher's biggest hit in over a decade. It also sparked a resurgence in her career, with her subsequent album "Heart of Stone" selling over 4 million copies worldwide.

But it wasn't just the song that catapulted Cher back into the limelight. It was also her bold and daring music video for "If I Could Turn Back Time." In the video, she wore a revealing outfit and danced on a battleship, causing quite a stir and generating a lot of media attention.

Cher's comeback was not just about the music, it was also about her image. She showed the world that she was not afraid to take risks and be herself, even if it meant going against societal norms and expectations.

Her comeback was a testament to her resilience and determination. She refused to let a career slump define her and instead used it as an opportunity to reinvent herself and come back stronger than ever.

**Key Takeaway:** Cher's comeback with "If I Could Turn Back Time" teaches us that setbacks and challenges are not the end, but rather a chance to grow and come back even stronger. It also reminds us to stay true to ourselves and not be afraid to take risks and be different.

# Chapter 7

*Philanthropy and Humanitarian Work*

Cher was not only a talented singer and actress, but she was also a kind and compassionate person. Throughout her career, she has used her fame and fortune to help those in need. Let's take a closer look at Cher's philanthropy and humanitarian work.

One of Cher's biggest passions is helping children in need. She has been a long-time supporter of the Children's Craniofacial Association, which helps children with facial deformities. Cher has also donated millions of dollars to the Intrepid Fallen Heroes Fund, which supports military personnel and their families.

In addition to her monetary donations, Cher has also been actively involved in humanitarian efforts. In 1985, she organized a benefit concert for the victims of the Armenian earthquake, raising over $10 million. She also founded the Cher Charitable Foundation, which supports various causes such as AIDS research and victims of natural disasters.

But Cher's philanthropy doesn't stop there. She has also been a strong advocate for animal rights. In 1990, she helped establish the Cher Institute for Environmental Studies at the California State University, Northridge. The institute focuses on environmental issues and animal welfare.

In 2008, Cher received the Audrey Hepburn Humanitarian Award for her tireless efforts in philanthropy and humanitarian work. She has also been

honored with the GLAAD Vanguard Award
for her support of the LGBTQ+ community.

**Key Takeaway:** Cher's philanthropy
and humanitarian work shows us that no
matter how successful we are, we should
always use our platform to help those in
need. Even small acts of kindness can make
a big difference in someone's life.

# Chapter 8

*Las Vegas Residency and Continued*

*Success*

Cher's career was on fire. She had conquered the music industry with her powerful voice and electrifying performances. But she wasn't done yet. In 2008, at the age of 62, Cher embarked on a new adventure - a Las Vegas residency.

Las Vegas, also known as the Entertainment Capital of the World, is home to some of the most iconic performers in history. And now, Cher was joining their ranks. She signed a three-year contract with Caesars Palace, one of the most prestigious hotels on the Las Vegas strip.

The show, titled "Cher at the Colosseum," was a massive production with elaborate costumes, dazzling choreography, and of course, Cher's signature hits. It was a spectacle that wowed audiences night after night.

Cher's residency was a huge success, selling out almost every show. Fans from all over the world flocked to Las Vegas to see the legendary performer in action. And Cher didn't disappoint. She gave it her all, belting out her biggest hits like "Believe," "If I Could Turn Back Time," and "I Got You Babe."

But it wasn't just the music that captivated the audience. Cher also shared personal stories and anecdotes, giving fans a glimpse into her life and career. She even brought her mother, Georgia Holt, on stage for a special duet.

The Las Vegas residency was a turning point in Cher's career. It proved that she was not just a one-hit wonder, but a true icon with staying power. Her performances were praised by critics and fans alike, solidifying her status as a music legend.

After her successful run in Las Vegas, Cher continued to tour and perform around the world. She released new music, collaborated with other artists, and even starred in a Broadway musical based on her life. At the age of 73, she shows no signs of slowing down.

**Key Takeaway:** Cher's Las Vegas residency showed that age is just a number when it comes to talent and success. It also taught us the importance of reinventing ourselves and trying new things, even if we have already achieved great success.

# Chapter 9

## Iconic Fashion and Style

Cher was not only known for her incredible singing and acting abilities, but also for her iconic fashion and style. From the 1960s to the present day, Cher has been a fashion icon and trendsetter, constantly pushing boundaries and challenging traditional fashion norms.

In the 1960s, Cher and her then-husband Sonny Bono rose to fame with their hit song "I Got You Babe." During this time, Cher's fashion sense was heavily influenced by the popular mod style of the era. She could often be seen wearing mini skirts, go-go boots, and colorful patterns.

As the 1970s rolled around, Cher's style evolved into a more bohemian and hippie look. She embraced flowy dresses, bell-bottom pants, and long, wavy hair. Her fashion choices reflected the free-spirited and carefree attitude of the decade.

But it wasn't until the 1980s that Cher truly cemented her status as a fashion icon. With her daring and avant-garde style, she pushed boundaries and challenged traditional gender norms. She famously wore a revealing black bodysuit with a leather jacket and fishnet stockings for her performance of "If I Could Turn Back Time" at the 1989 Video Music Awards. This outfit caused quite a stir and solidified Cher as a fashion risk-taker.

In the 1990s, Cher continued to make bold fashion statements, often incorporating elements of glamour and luxury into her looks. She was often seen wearing designer gowns and extravagant accessories, showcasing her love for high-end fashion.

Even in her later years, Cher has continued to impress with her fashion choices. She has embraced a more sophisticated and elegant style, while still maintaining her unique flair. From sparkling sequin dresses to chic pantsuits, Cher has proven that age is just a number when it comes to fashion.

**Key Takeaway:** Cher's iconic fashion and style have been a reflection of her bold and fearless personality. She has continuously pushed boundaries and challenged traditional fashion norms, inspiring others to embrace their own unique sense of style.

# Chapter 10

*Legacy and Impact on Pop Culture*

Cher was not only a talented singer and actress, but she also left a lasting legacy on pop culture. Her impact can still be seen and felt today, even though she first rose to fame over 50 years ago.

One of the ways Cher has influenced pop culture is through her iconic fashion choices. From her daring and revealing outfits on stage to her glamorous red carpet looks, Cher was always pushing boundaries and setting trends. Her style has been emulated by countless artists and fashionistas, and her influence can be seen in today's fashion industry.

But it wasn't just her fashion that made Cher a pop culture icon. She was also known for her unique and powerful voice, which has inspired generations of singers. Her songs, such as "Believe" and "If I Could Turn Back Time," have become timeless classics and are still played on the radio today. Cher's music has transcended generations and continues to be loved by people of all ages.

In addition to her music and fashion, Cher's impact on pop culture can also be seen in her acting career. She starred in numerous films, including "Moonstruck" and "Mermaids," and won an Academy Award for her role in "Moonstruck." Her performances were always captivating and she brought a sense of authenticity to every character she played.

Cher's legacy also extends beyond her own career. She has been a vocal advocate for LGBTQ+ rights and has used her platform to raise awareness and support for various causes. She has also been a strong supporter of women's rights and has inspired many young girls to follow their dreams and break barriers.

**Key Takeaway:** Cher's impact on pop culture is undeniable. From her fashion choices to her music and acting career, she has left a lasting legacy that continues to inspire and influence artists and fans alike. Her fearless attitude and determination to be true to herself have made her an icon for generations to come.

# Dear Reader,

*Thank you for choosing "Little Big Giant - Stories of Wisdom and Inspiration"! We hope this book has inspired and motivated you on your own journey to success.*

*If you enjoyed reading this book and believe in the power of its message, we kindly ask for your support. Please consider leaving a positive review on the platform where you purchased the book. Your review will help spread the message to more young readers, empowering them to dream big and achieve greatness. We acknowledge that mistakes can happen, and we appreciate your forgiveness.*

*Remember, the overall message of this book is the key. Thank you for being a part of our mission to inspire and uplift young minds.*

Made in the USA
Middletown, DE
04 November 2024